SKANDALON

Southern Messenger Poets
Dave Smith, Series Editor

SKANDALON

POEMS

T. R. HUMMER

Louisiana State University Press)|(*Baton Rouge*

Published by Louisiana State University Press
Copyright © 2014 by T. R. Hummer
All rights reserved
Manufactured in the United States of America
LSU Press Paperback Original
First printing

Designer: Michelle A. Neustrom
Typefaces: Whitman, text; Penumbra MM, display

The author gratefully acknowledges publication of many of the poems in this book in the
following journals: *Blackbird; Catch Up; Codex; Common-Place; Cutthroat; diode; Faultline;*
the *Kenyon Review; Mantis; Mary: A Journal of New Writing; Miramar; The New Yorker;*
Plume; The Rumpus; Slate; This Corner; White Stag.

Library of Congress Cataloging-in-Publication Data

Hummer, T. R.
   [Poems. Selections]
   Skandalon : poems / T.R. Hummer.
      pages cm — (Southern messenger poets)
   ISBN 978-0-8071-5741-1 (pbk. : alk. paper) — ISBN 978-0-8071-5742-8 (pdf) —
ISBN 978-0-8071-5743-5 (epub) — ISBN 978-0-8071-5744-2 (mobi)
   I. Title.
   PS3558.U445S53 2015
   811'.54—dc23

                                                      2014000861

For Theo and Jackson
and Beth

Our divisions are a *Skandalon*, a stumbling block, a snare, and a trap, an evidence of our disobedience.

—RICHARD JOHN NEUHAUS

Any particular "Thou" may become a skandalon at any time.

—H. A. HODGES, *Journal of Theological Studies*

He who has suffer'd you to impose on him, knows you.

—WILLIAM BLAKE

CONTENTS

SKANDALON

THE LOVERS' BOOK OF THE DEAD

In the metro tunnels of a strange city where every sign
    is in a tongue not hers, and no one understands
Her questions, she steps at random into a crowded car
    and disembarks on a wasted plateau, just at the snowline
Where an oxcart full of children prepares for departure,
    and two old women argue the logistics of provision.
Years ago he told her he would wait for her here. He drifted on
    before her, but only just so far. Now she appropriates his hand
And they set out barefoot over the naked ice, a thousand
    years ahead of them, a moment, nothing, their path obscure
And irrelevant in the twilight, vanishing into a future of entanglement
    to the north, where a broken glacier grinds its own enjambments
Against themselves with a sound like sexual thunder.

VICTIMS OF THE WEDDING 1
Prenuptial

He wakes with his face pressed against the window of an airliner. Outside he can see nothing but clouds, and in his memory the dream he had been dreaming also contained nothing but clouds. There was, he thinks, a rightness in that marriage of world and dream, of mind and sky: Adam's dream of Eve in Milton, which the man had read in college. He is holding an old spiral-bound notebook in his lap, with the nub of a pencil attached to it by a length of greasy string. Should he be writing something? Was he in the habit of taking notes? As he watches, the thunderheads through which the plane is flying seem to be vanishing, thinning, or melting away. Soon he will see the earth again, and the city to which he is traveling; soon he will remember himself, and the name of the city, and the reason he is going there. But the more the clouds depart, the less he can see the ground; gaps in the clouds reveal only darkness, and darkness beyond darkness, until at length he begins to see stars within it, and he thinks *Have I slept into the night? But wasn't I to arrive at noon?* Were others on the airplane seeing what he saw? Was there a general bewilderment, or panic? He looks down at his notebook and sees written there, in his own hand, these words: *Do you hear the sound the water in the streambed makes as it runs over smooth stones? There is the entrance.* He looks around and sees there is no one else on the plane. The seats are empty, as though while he was sleeping there had been an evacuation, or the Rapture had taken the others. Beyond the window he can see now only space and its unfamiliar constellations. The clouds had erased the earth. *So,* he thinks, *this is how it ends.* But isn't he supposed to attend a wedding? What will they think of him, the bride and groom, the wedding party, the bridesmaids, if he does not appear? How will he explain himself? And how will his gift now be delivered?

THROMBOSIS

Bits of the body migrate: bone dust
    from the crematorium, gasses
Leached from graves. But in the body
    itself, there is other breakage. The journey
Through that labyrinth is perilous.
    There are stations. *None passes*
Declares the angel with a sword of flame
    at the duodenum's portal. But the great
Black gate of the heart stands open.
    Enter, particle, and begin.

HUND'S RULE

Each orbital in a subshell must contain an electron
before a second electron can be added.
—FRIEDRICH HUND

If there is not one present already, none may enter.
    Where three are gathered, let it be known that nothing exists.
The children cannot be left alone, nor can their great-grandfather.

Twins, the boys would not assay the dark hall if they were not together.
    The old man, they remember, sat in his office honing his lists.
If there is not one present already, none may enter.

Years he plotted metaphorical murder, pillage, and empire.
    Now he rocks in the parlor, drooling, waiting to be kissed.
The children cannot be left alone, nor can their great-grandfather,

Nor can trusties on a chain gang, kleptomaniacs, or houseguests. Either
    You may determine speed or position; both, never. Case dismissed.
If there is not one present already, none may enter,

But neither may anyone leave, whether singly or together.
    Stars refer to their heaven, a swarm of guardian asterisks.
The children cannot be left alone, nor can their great-grandfather.

Half dead, he will not die; half grown, they are smaller and meaner.
    Nonexistent gods consider this paradox, thoroughly unimpressed.
The children cannot be left alone, nor can their great-grandfather:
    If there is not one present already, none may enter.

TEXT

The blues pianist's bleeding hands trace calligraphy on the keys.
    This too is art. And the rabbi's prayer on the killing floor.
Ritual slaughter is known as *shechita*. The knife is called a *chalef.*
    In Samoan, *ta* means *to strike,* and hence *tattoo,*
And the attendant percussion of wooden implements.
    This too is music. And the double paradiddle
Of ordnance in Afghanistan. Meanwhile, in the penal colony
    The harrow writes on a man until he is dead:
The tip of a large iron needle had gone through his forehead.
    You hold a book serenely in your hand: it is a gift,
It is *techne,* many human lives have been grotesquely crushed
    so that you may sit quietly with it in your chair
While the cat purrs in the crook of your arm. Outside,
    moonlight lays down its pentatonic line.
The bright chisel of language descends in your brain.
    This too is an instrument. This too is a tool.

VICTIMS OF THE WEDDING 2
The Doorjamb of the Labyrinth

An angel and a daemon were having a meeting just past midnight on a dewy lawn. They were the angel and daemon of a particular woman and man—or *one* of their angels and *one* of their daemons—and they had business to attend to.

We have both made promises, the daemon said. *Whose promises shall be kept?*

My promises, said the angel, *are difficult things, but attainable.*

Mine, said the daemon, *are easy things, but impossible.*

That's the traditional way, the angel said, and they shook hands on it.

MILK

It was a temple of the dark sublime with high-speed elevators
    that lifted us—O lyric lift—to the ninety-seventh level.
Our cubicles resembled milking stalls in an agribusiness dairy
    where the farmhands—call them that, though their job descriptions
Said *Lactic Technicians*—are what they always were. I remember
    the mauled one whose left arm, ripped off by a sorghum cutter,
Was prone to beat his children while he was sleeping; and the woman
    whose face was eclipsed by a malignant shadow of birthmark—
She saw small devils twisting the hydraulic valves of the giant
    chrome tank in the milk-room. The foreman was the normal one;
He kept an eye on us all, but carried a pistol in the small of his back—
    For rats, he muttered with a sidelong maniac grin. Then there were the cattle:
They queued up continually at the barn door mooing for us to service
    their animal needs: food in, milk out, and cycle away the shit,
But they dreamed of liquid nitrogen, the tanks of sperm in a distant room,
    harvested from the bovine elite and stored like platinum: capital,
You might say, flowing from its mystical font into the bloodline
    of nonstop traffic, newsstands, a Cartier's branch on the corner,
The far field of Times Square, sterilized now, the great political hosing
    well in the past, occluded by the digital billboard: Got Milk?

POST-AMERICAN

Bougainvillea and Tuscan tile on the patio, sunset composed above the lake.
Between one altar and the other is interposed a southering flock of monarchs.
There's a chair for a daemon at the table. There's a residue of genius on the lawn.
A black streak mars the driveway brick: someone peeled rubber and was gone.
A shadow in the orangery echoes a shadow on the croquet court
Where a wedge of colored balls points to the shadow of a rusting golf cart.
Up the stone walkway, the empty fountain holds an empty pigeon's nest
Within which bits of eggshell are *memento mori* of a form, erased.
They are gone to offices and classrooms, to the factory and the killing floor,
To the florist, to the hospice, to the bank, to the barn, to be burnt, to be blind,
    to be born,
And lizards sun on the patio stone where the skull of a cat gives its stare—
Desperate and worshipful, hopeless, starved, permanent, and alone—
Waiting for someone to finally come home from making and being made,
Or for gods to gyre on the water again and settle rough on the blasted esplanade.

THE DECLINE EFFECT

She went on four legs at morning into the Marketplace
  of the Virgins. She bought potatoes and an onion
And the tail of an ox for soup. The fountains of the forum
  healed every supplicant. She watched a crippled girl
Strap on marble legs, and a foaming politician
  cough up a herd of swine. All shadows shrank.
She stood straighter as the archbishop untied her tunic.
  At noon they talked over glasses of grappa and The Holy
Father described to her the mechanism of the erosion of truth
  in the inner sanctum. Outside, twilight arrived
Like an epilogue. She waited in the proscenium, tail forgotten,
  for the last bus to her distant neighborhood, depending
On her cane to support her there in her well-earned habit.

VICTIMS OF THE WEDDING 3
A Confusion of Choices among the Forking Ways

She went down to the shore of her lake, and there she found him, naked and unconscious, washed up among the remnants of his craft that had foundered. She lifted him easily—she was powerful—and took him back to her home. She laid him still unconscious on her bed, and washed him all over, cleansing every inch of him carefully, considering each part. *This one has promise*, she thought, *and so I won't turn him immediately into a pig, unless he turns out to be one.* She washed him again—not because she thought he needed it, but for her own curiosity and satisfaction, probing into every crevice of him. *When he wakes*, she thought, *if he ever does, I will find out his story. But for now I will find out him.* And she washed him a third time, anointing him in costly oils after absorbing every smell he possessed.

The angel and the daemon sat near the bed in their usual chairs. *This is an interesting scenario*, the angel said, *though I have a feeling I have seen it before.*

What haven't *you seen before?* the daemon said, and then went on watching while she washed the senseless man a fourth time for reasons entirely of her own.

THE LOVER

Across the room a woman is talking to someone.
    Her focus on the other is complete; her eyes
Are fixed on the eyes of the one to whom she speaks
    almost prayerfully, as though with her words
She washes the feet of the Beloved, as if her speech
    is the long hair with which she wipes them dry.
The intensity of her gaze, the eloquence of her gestures,
    make it unimportant that no one stands facing her,
That she talks into empty air, that she stares into a wall
    like someone insane. The tiny cell phone
Attached to her ear excuses her, but fails to explain
    how the greatness of her passion creates a form
In the nothingness before her, and how everyone envies
    the one to whom she is speaking, how all of us
Desire to be the one thus re-created.

ANOTHER HORIZONTAL LYRIC

The yellow ball stays where the boy has thrown it,
    stalled in the air inches from the nose
Of a leaping border collie who hangs a foot
    above the ground. The boy's arm is stuck
At a characteristic angle, cantilevered. In a lawn chair
    his mother holds the brush that will never reach her toenail,
One drop of pink levitating just above her skin.
    So many cars immobilized. A lawn mower founders,
Fountaining green. And in a dark bedroom, a woman
    hesitates forever above the transfixed body
Of a lover, seized up for the incoming stroke.
    Time is a mercy of completion, our nerves
Going up in meaningless smoke, our animal hearts released.

OOO BABY BABY

Across a darkness that might be water, cheap paper lanterns burn,
    and their faint luminescence is a distraction from the thought
That if there is no water there, sweetheart, we are screwed—unresolved
    darkness being just *that* problematic. But no, it must be water,
Must be that lake just outside of town, because listen, there is music playing,
    and so there must be crepe paper streamers and a bowl of grim punch,
Bags of potato chips—god we hope so—and, in the unsustainable light
    of the pavilion, couples dancing. We might still have that kind of hope
After we die. We might find ourselves in our bodiless bafflement, hanging
    above the expanse of nonbeing, thinking *water,* thinking *dancers*—
And Smokey Robinson surrounds us with his voice, another miracle: the old
    prom dream, *I might get lucky,* just one more angel among the tiny lights.

VICTIMS OF THE WEDDING 4
An Uncertain Path through Branching Tunnels

In the middle of the night he finally wakes up. He is lying next to a woman, who is sleeping; it is winter, and there is a deep fresh snowfall outside; though there are no lights on, the window is illuminated by moonlight reflected from the snow. The man and woman are both naked, but covered in a thick duvet they are warm. The man's arms are around the woman and her back is to him; he can feel her breath as it moves in and out of her body, just as he himself had done a few hours earlier, she atop him and astride, but with the cover up against the cold that surrounded them, leaning close to him so he could take her nipple in his mouth and feel the soft moan that came out of her along with her breath, the same breath he can see lit like the window by moonlight, snow-light, that hangs around them, like the cold that hangs around them, making a crystal cave for them in the bed where they lie, as in a cave in a forest, safe and glowing just a little, magical, alive.

WHITMAN'S PANTRY

Dried beans in a muslin sack, tied shut with greasy string.
    An ounce of ginger root to brew *digestif,*
Procured on physician's advice from an "Oriental" grocer
    at remarkable expense, desiccated now almost
Past recognition. Half a pound of sowbelly wrapped
    in cheesecloth. Hard cheese. A licorice twist.
A box of sugar cubes to meliorate bitter tea—with these
    you could construct a model of the odd granite tomb
He insisted on for his own final habitation.
    There in his beloved Camden he rests in a blank box.
You may count there twelve thoracic vertebrae,
    two lunate bones, two trapeziums, a coccyx,
And all the rest, to the final mystic number *two hundred and six.*
    His book is a homemade Bible. His tomb is a homemade Blake.
Here is the skull-cup that held the brain his doctors lifted.
    He was the catalog of his perfect body. In love with health,
He ate grim food. Behold his ounce of flour, cut with weevils.
    Behold his dried orange peel, studded with a sorry clove.
This pantry is a compost now. It is small; it contains millipedes.
    The bottom shelf reveals this lunar dust, a Kosmos in it
Writ in groceries. *Here,* as he never said. I hold it toward you.

CERTAIN SLANT

Concertina music breaks its foam on the haberdashery window,
    a murder ballad so old even the monkey knows the words
And spits them one by one into the tin cup he tritely holds.
    Who has a monkey these days? Who dares make a monkey dance?
But people are busy with their shopping. They have argyle socks on
    their minds. Four hundred miles to the south-southwest
Caissons hulk through Gettysburg. But on this Amherst street
    the shadow of a small, thin cloud dissipates over horse carts.
And still the concertina plays its monotonous music, another
    familiar melody. Common meter, common meter, common meter.
"The Yellow Rose of Texas," it might be singing, or "Amazing Grace."
    The whole town is embedded in the amber of that rhythm.

POISONOUS PERSONA

I, Fernando Pessoa, am not myself, and never was. Pour me another absinthe,
    de Campos, and I will pour one for you. Pour me another soul.
You might say that when I was born they left my bedroom door open, if by "open
    bedroom door" is understood a metaphor for metempsychosis.
Or you might say that my birth was the fanfare for the end of the personal ownership
    of selfhood, that I was born a metaphysical communist
And stand ready to die a dedicated drunk. Is absinthe drunk in Portugal? Do persons
    live there, distinct from one another, freestanding?
The problem with Portugal is that it is a flat character in the drama of Europe.
    Look at England, look at France: they stand before us whole—
But here we are a beehive of probabilities. One of my heteronyms, for instance,
    has invented the Absinthe Clock that measures half-lives,
The shorter the better. It works only on Portuguese soil, and sometimes in Brazil,
    but in Spain it grinds and wheezes and pukes out Quixotes
Like pater nosters. Quixote was Quixote, and he is ubiquitous always as himself,
    just as the Pope tends to be the Pope, or absinthe absinthe.
But I, Fernando Pessoa, am not myself, alone am not myself and am never alone,
    with so many indistinguishable others inhabiting the mental avenue
Where I walk from the office after a day of translating myself into the terrible prose
    of salesmen, to the bar and the shadow of my absinthe.

VICTIMS OF THE WEDDING 5
Dead End

A spring night next. He is standing at the top of the garden's highest hill just as the sun is setting: a very slender crescent moon, no more than a curved incision of light, presides over the sun's departure. The air is heavy with smells: cut grass, fresh herbs, the provocation of mock orange. The man feels himself pierced by the evening's aura: it is a bounty and a judgment of which he feels unworthy but by which he feels blessed. When the woman appears soundlessly beside him as if herself conjured by that air, or as if the embodiment of that aura, he is not surprised. The hill is hers, and the sky is hers, and the night, and the moon carved into it. This place is like a flawless piece of fruit, into which he has insinuated himself like rot, but he is neither sorry nor guilty; rather he is grateful to be so nourished. *Is it time?* he asks the woman. *Time for what?* She says. *To die,* he says, *or to go inside.*

SAPPHO

Whether it's really an island is any-
    one's guess, but the ocean is black as far as
The mainland, and the mainland is crumbling in-
    to the water. She swims

To music that no musician is playing
    and will never be sung and will never be
Written—the music of consciousness, purer
    than water or sky

Or the body that carries the lyric for-
    ward forever in silence that only the
Body can bear (*bear over* sings metaphor)
    on or off islands

Where once the woman reclaims her nothingness,
    and only the osprey watches the tidal
Grinding of earthliness, no consciousness cares
    what any music means.

AGNOSTICISM

Because nobody knows, he stands at the trailhead watching
    a hawk torture a pigeon against the empty sky.
The pigeon is a dumb, lumbering thing. The hawk will kill it
    with an exquisite slowness that is the luxury of power.
It is not possible to hope the pigeon will win: it cannot win,
    but he cannot even want it to, such a rat with wings:
And there is the first failure of empathy. It is not enough
    to say the hawk prevails because it is beautiful.
It prevails because it is swift and merciless, and nature has made
    certain we regard the swift and merciless as beautiful.
But already the sky has emptied. Thought is so slow, so torturous
    that the stain it makes in desert sunlight lingers
After the talon strikes and the aura vanishes.

TRANSCENDENTAL

From what the wind wrote
    in the wheat field she took a little hope;
That rippling prosody seemed to promise to give up
    meaning like tea leaves in a cup.

Likewise when her lovers' unshaven faces
    inscribed their stories on her lips
She almost understood. A universe nearly legible
    expressed her. If only she knew Braille. If only she had taste.

VICTIMS OF THE WEDDING 6
Backtrack/Recursion I

In the back of the house there is a secret room. No one knows about it, not the man, not even the woman whose house it is; likely not even the previous owner had known of its existence, or the owner before that one. The history of the room goes back to the builder of the house, and even *she,* by the end of her life, barely remembered it was there. It had been, then, decades since anyone had found the cunningly hidden door, or opened its intricate catch, much less entered the room to find its secret. Or such was the dream the man is having when he wakes that morning, at the same time the woman wakes, saying *I had the strangest dream about a room at the back of the house. . . .*

THE NIETZSCHE HORSE

There were two crazy men, the one with the whip and the one with the huge
    moustache: they were dancing together, no, they were fighting
When the eyes of the whipless one brightened: sometimes that happens when
    you bite someone, or when you're fucking: people become disturbed
When horses fuck: to them, I think, it's like mountains fucking: things
    that big ought to keep it to themselves. The idiot man with the whip
Tore his hand away then, and hit me with the little crop—you think that hurt?
    I'm a horse!—But the other man began dancing again, moustache
Covered with foam—what *was* that? had he run too far?—and he was muttering
    in that barbaric way humans have, sounds like *Bismarck* and *German*
And even the man with the whip was becoming frightened, or awestruck,
    or maybe he looked like that because he was hungry, it's hard to tell
About humans, and I was losing interest anyway, a hay wagon was passing,
    it was much less boring than the weeping man with his arms
Around my neck suddenly, or the moron with the whip—if he'd been a horse,
    he'd have died at birth—moaning *God,* and the other suddenly
Laughing like a jackal and saying *Fool, you have no notion who you're talking to.*

GALL THEMSELVES, AND GASH

That hawk-shaped shadow, Hopkins, is God's homage to you.
  Give beauty back, you said, and God listened, though God is dead,
And you are dead, and no one knows what that means, or whether you care—
  but it is likely, though not proven, that you don't hear
The music of what happens from the heaven of nothing where you are.
  We spend our lives talking to the deaf dead until we join them.
But over the desert, out of sight, something moves and throws its darkness
  down to us: like salvation? like a frayed lifeline? like the bent,
Corroded coin a king's servant tosses from a coach to a leper?
  The priesthood of mortality is conferred upon us all,
Even the hawk—though she is indifferent, except that she smells
  the rich black blood of the desert rat, and hungers, and heels, and falls.

THE DEATH OF NERUDA

A subterranean enjambment, a pure minor
    triad blown on a crude Aeolian harp
Strung by a peasant grandmother
    and hung from a plane-tree bough
On the edge of a field of flax—the perfect blue
    of the flowers unfurled for the phalanx
Of bees that must surely be coming, but not
    yet, for something at the margin of the field
Grinds so perilously we can barely hear
    the music we know is there even as it is being
Erased forever from our pre-memories, cut
    from our amygdala so sudden and so clean
That we are no longer who we were, or anything
    else, and never again can be, and will not care,
And will not think of the blitzed white towers
    of hives where honey and rainwater
Mix slowly in a poisonous final solution.

VICTIMS OF THE WEDDING 7
Recursion II

She wanted to be naked in starlight on the jetty that went out over the small lake; she left her clothes in a neat pile at the very end, where the weathered wood overhung the water, and stood feeling the warm air against her body. She wanted to be naked in starlight there, and she was, and it was good. She wanted him to be naked with her, and he left his clothes too in a less neat pile and stood feeling her feeling the warm air against her body; she wanted him to be naked in starlight there, and he was, and it was good. She wanted him to lie down on the wood, and he did, carefully, not to get splinters, and she stood above him, watching him, wanting him to be naked in starlight—and he became naked starlight to satisfy her wanting. She wanted starlight to be naked in her on the jetty, and her will was done. And he? He wanted her will to be done.

POE ON BROADWAY

in memoriam J. D. Salinger

He could not hold it against the bird that it shat,
    copiously and often but unpredictably—
Lacking a sphincter, it had no choice—
    but its moodiness and outbursts
Of viciousness were harder to forgive. While it
    could not take off a finger, like certain parrots,
That beak was dangerous, and he had the scars
    to prove it. It rode his shoulder
Like a miasma of depression—it was a raven,
    it had a role, a tradition to uphold—and he walked
The city, from boardinghouse to subway to diner,
    bearing an imposed symbolic predisposition
To gloom. A talking raven was a common idea, one
    explained implicitly by the role it played: it must seem
Like natural supernaturalism for a black bird on a shoulder
    to utter its lugubrious trisyllable. In truth, his raven
Could not talk—he had tried to teach it and failed, perhaps
    because he could not bring himself to split
Its tongue—and so had himself learned ventriloquism,
    which the bird consented to accompany
By opening and closing its beak on a secret signal.
    That was all it took to make a modest stipend
If you were content to live alone in a cardboard box
    down the throat of a blind alley, with a shitting bird
For a neighbor. It was a living. Each morning on his corner—
    a good spot on Broadway no less, that he'd swindled
From a juggler—he'd set his tip jar down.
    It might take an hour for his repeated riff to catch
An ear, especially on busy weekdays, given the traffic noise,
    but always sooner or later, someone would lift

An eyebrow, pause for a moment, smile or not, and drop
Something into the jar. This was the routine
For years, and he never ceased to be surprised
no one inquired, ever, how the thing was done.

PAUL CELAN IN PARIS

What was it Heidegger wrote? Everybody wondered.
　　The words were plain on the page,
But the sense of that German prose would break a skull.
　　Past midnight, Antschel struggled with the massive book.
Do not imagine he did not know the Philosopher
　　was a Nazi. He marked the obvious lines
With a marginalized six-pointed star. He could feel
　　the book burning itself, its ashen pages yielding
A crematorium pollution. The Jew in him attended,
　　with the greatest care. The Jew in him? What
Was he thinking? Had he become a prison? The Philosopher's
　　German strung its concertina wire around the bedroom.
Soon everyone would die of it, soon everyone's
　　name would change. Retranslate: *Dasein. The Seine.*

CORROSIVE LYRIC

The fly that dissolves in the carnivorous pitcher
    of the bog plant; the bog, which breaks down
Tigers' bones but tans and supples their hides;
    the lump of ore wasted to sand by acid rain;
And the old man smoking at his corner desk
    who has burned himself alive with poetry.

VICTIMS OF THE WEDDING 8
Sense of Direction

The angel and the daemon sat beside the bed where the man and woman were making love. They were interested in human lovemaking, always—connoisseurs, one might say, though they had no direct experience of it—and found it interesting to compare notes on the process.

Do you think, the angel said, *that what they're doing there is really worth all the effort they put into it? It seems to be a lot of work.*

I take them at their word, the daemon said, *and in every word they speak, even when they are not speaking, they affirm the worth of it.*

But look, the angel said, *he pierces her. How can that be a pleasant thing?*

It's a mystery, the daemon said, *but she pierces him too. The mystery resides in that also.*

But can it be a pleasure to be licked like that? He's licking her nipples. I do not see the joy in that.

And soon, said the daemon, *her tongue will be in his ear. Our understanding of their ecstasy is quite beside the point. Just accept that.*

You seem to be implying, the angel went on, *that there is a reciprocity in it?*

Otherwise, the daemon told him, *they would both be terribly lonely right now.*

The woman grasped the man's hair and pulled his head to her mouth just as he pressed deep inside her; she put her tongue in his ear and he moaned, but she whispered to him, *Are those two still watching us?*

He glanced over out of the corner of his eye, where the two supernatural gargoyles sat on three-legged stools beside the bed. *They are,* he said. *And does it excite you to have them watch us?*

If it didn't, she said, feeling her turbulence beginning, *they would both be terribly lonely right now.*

TOOL & DIE

In the final unburdening, massive crates are moved
    from vehicle to loading dock into the labyrinth
Of the terminal, where synchronized forklifts reenact
    the marriage of Heaven and Hell. Let it all go.
It's a heavy freight you've carried. *It's a long, lonesome road*
    the soundtrack sang, road music on your inner radio.
The body has its weigh and wants to use it
    till it's time. Unload. The warehouse of the snow
Is empty, pilgrim, the invoice blank, its spaces oblivious
    to the lathe, the jig, the torch, the grinding wheel.

WESTBOUND

Little Cat Feet

A universe of near-unendurable suffering, in which our fate
    is to receive pain rejoicingly in order to receive more pain.
The man in the light rail car is bleeding from the chin.
    By now it's just an ooze, but his face and shirt are stained.
There is something—what?—*peculiar* about his cheerfulness,
    an electrical storm rolling over the prairie of his hippocampus.
What do you do for a living, he asks, and, told, asks it again.
    I'm bloody, he says. *Bicycle.* And he points where it hangs
From a rack. *It's mine. I'm restoring it. What do you do for a living?*
    I like poems. This one's my favorite: The cat comes in
On little cat feet. *You know it? The cat comes in.* The bicycle
    hangs perfect on the rack, dusty, but well oiled and functional.
Restoration? The arc of our lives carries us forward, its pace
    controlled by an invisible metronome. He says that boys
Laughed at him when he fell. *I said Fuck You. What do you do*
    for a living? His hands worry the thickening blood
On his neck. *I like that poem too,* I say, *but it's fog: the fog comes in*
    on little cat feet. He frowns, thinking. *Yes,* he says, *the cat*
Comes in on little cat feet, and he slouches his shoulders, arms out,
    creeping in the air. *See? It makes an image in my mind.*
When the prophet Elisha entered Bethel, the little children
    mocked his baldness, and, the Bible tells us, *he turned back,*
And looked on them, and cursed them in the name of the Lord.
    And there came forth two she-bears out of the wood, and tore
Forty and two children of them. His bloodied hands shake.
    We are going somewhere. It makes an image in my mind.

EASTBOUND
The Book of Enoch

We recognize the man with the whip by his smell, even in the dead
    of night, as we call it, even when we sleep, as we say,
Like a stone: he enters our dream and the stink of his sweat
    wakes us just before the flagrum comes down, commuters
On the platform driven, train driven. The world is burning,
    Heraclitus wrote. East, the great desert takes the lash
Of solar flares. The man in the window seat is not perspiring.
    A leather bag and a bottle of water rest in his perfect khaki lap.
I have resumed the studies I started years ago, he says; *I investigate the angels*
    who are everywhere around us. The aisles of this train are full of them,
And the platforms at the stations; some of us in these seats are angels.
    His face behind his sunglasses is serene as the train rolls smoothly.
In the ancient book, canonical in Ethiopia, the angels lusted
    after the daughters of women. They made a pact of silence
And fathered a race of giants, who prospered and devoured the earth.
    My grandfather learned this from adepts in Addis Ababa:
We must love everyone and be kind to every stranger, lest we offend God's agents.
    Beyond the horizon there is a great mechanical quaking,
The gears of the Imperium grinding into a corrosive bronze dust.
    And there I saw One who had a head of days, and His head was white
like wool. And we recognize him because he punishes us for our inconstancy—
    we are not faithful to our Being like the stones or the fruits of trees.
Therefore shall ye execrate your days, and the years of your life shall perish,
    ye shall be blown across your desert lives like tumbleweed
Before the Mercedes-Benz, ye shall enter into office buildings weeping
    and drive yourselves, and marry, and suffer the everlasting scourge.

VICTIMS OF THE WEDDING 9
Recursion III

The woman lit a candle, and then with her finger drew a shape in the air. The man appeared there.

Of all the women in the world, he said, *I invoke you.*

I thought it was I who had conjured you here, she said.

So it always seems to humans, the daemon instructed the angel, *at all times and everywhere.*

TERRORISM

Black wavelets lap against pilings. Bone dust settles on the pier.
    The ferryman looks up from his tiller at a man in an Armani suit
Who steps out of the shadows, swinging his briefcase, staggering a little
    before stopping at the edge of the jetty, knowing—despite the absence
Of his head (and the eyes in that head) and despite the hole in his chest
    from which an ichor, the ghost of blood, fountains in the wake of the
        bomb-blast—
That the wine-dark water is perilous, being neither wine nor water.

TRAPPIST

The old monk has not spoken a word in decades,
    and would he remember how if he wanted to try?
There is temptation in the word *abyss,* or in *ex nihilo,*
    a whiff of sulfur in the trisyllabic *sacrament.*
And what if he stands looking at the blinding firmament
    where black holes megaphone the voice of God
In the ineffable traces of neutrinos? He might give voice
    To what he loves, if he could understand his own
Dialect, if he had a universe, or a mother, or a tongue.

SECOND NATURE

After the storm, a field of detritus chokes
    the bend in the river—tires from a junkyard,
A refrigerator door, limbs of deconstructed hardwoods.
    Turtles sun on the rusted flanks of oil drums.
A woman stands on a railed path above, her dog on a leash
    ambassadorial above the wreckage, nose quivering
At smells gathered from alien places, distances,
    the deaths of nameless creatures compounded
With gypsum and spores into an irresistible perfume
    which the human can only obliquely comprehend,
And therefore must be guarded fiercely, must be watched.

VICTIMS OF THE WEDDING 10
The Minotaur's Tracks

There was an inaudible, visceral rumbling in the night and the man and woman got up; they went out on the porch to see the cause. Down the hill, beyond the property line, there were explosions; spectral tanks raised their cannons in the starlight; concertina wire was strung across the road that ran by the house, and men and women wearing body armor maneuvered intricately and mysteriously in the middle distance. Meanwhile, people could be seen driving to work, walking their dogs, carrying bags of groceries past rows of foxholes; a minister performed a wedding next to a machine gun nest; children were playing, and shrapnel flew silently over the scene.

They're at it again, the woman said.

The last time this happened, we were killed, the man answered.

The woman put her arms around him and kissed him. *I think we'll be fine this time.*

When they came back inside, the angel and the daemon, who had been napping on their stools, leaning uncomfortably against each other, woke up. *Another war, eh,* the angel said. *Looks like it,* the daemon said, *but our two here don't seem worried.*

Why would they? the angel said. *Together they are stronger than an army.*

You think so? the daemon said. *Weren't they killed once before?*

Oh, my friend, said the angel, *even in their eternity things change, but never for the better or for the worse. They change because they change.*

ADORNMENT ON AN ANCIENT TOMB IN TIBET

They bear a venerable weight on poles balanced on their shoulders,
    the sum of their incarnations bundled in leather and tied
With thongs. Windblown snow makes their burden heavier.
    To compensate, they cast off memories. This side
Of the Mountain, the icepack is littered with stories
    left behind by other pilgrims. Traveler, you dare
Not touch them: they are poisonous histories
    of men and women frozen in tableaus of desire
And stranded forever in this wilderness. Shift the pain
    of the pole on your left shoulder. Stumble on.
The ice will come for you soon enough, blesséd one.

SHACKELTON'S BISCUIT

Of ox and luncheon tongue, six hundred pounds;
  of Wiltshire bacon, seven-tenths of a ton.
Seventeen hundred miles they walked, and it was
  pony meat that saved them. But one biscuit, this one
Of thousands, baked by Huntley & Palmers, a special formulation
  fortified with milk protein, survives—the men
Long dead, and the ponies, whose lives flew through
Bullet holes easily over the frozen labyrinth of the Fortuna Glacier,
  all gone to powder. Found a century later in the wrecked
Larder of one of Shackleton's way stations, it remains
  perfectly nutritious, and sold at a Christie's auction
Is worth a thousand-some sterling. *We had seen God in*
  His splendors; we had reached the naked soul of man,
He wrote. And: *This biscuit,* said a Christie's director,
  is an object that really catches the imagination.

THE LAST MEAL OF THE ICEMAN

He had eaten alpine ibex, which yields a greasy meat
    satisfying to a hunter, rich in fat that burns in the cells
Like napalm. He was dozing, his wrenched back propped
    against a boulder, when an arrowhead emerged
In his left shoulder, and his crazed skull limned a hatchet trauma.
    The tale of the CAT scan was suspect. Therefore the body,
Dead 5000 years, must rise and be broken again.
    Break bread with me. Break faith. Break down. Break in.
The ibex stood numinous on the snowy stone. That spring, the world
    was glacial, and the creature died in a fountain of blood
Freezing as it fell. He killed it for the body the others
    killed him for in turn. O hatchet, break the ice. Fossilized
In unconsciousness, he entered a different cold. Perhaps his soul
    waits in a purgatory like the meat locker of the afterlife,
Until a scalpel opens the stomach and the last meal is exhumed
    by unimaginable strangers with a basin and a clinical spoon.

VICTIMS OF THE WEDDING 11
A Hallway That Narrows to a Point

He was lost in a blizzard that went on for decades. He was immune, it seemed, to the cold of which it was an expression, but he could not see through it and he could not find his way out of it. After a while he stopped trying. It became his climate. He went about his life in spite of it, even forgetting, finally, that it was there. Without realizing it, he had become covered in snow, encased in it, and imagined that was his proper and fated condition. Within his snow skin he had a life. He did things, accomplished something. But he still dreamed, sometimes, of a spring field, of flowers in a vase, of orchids in a pot.

THE ART OF ALLEGORY

Dark smudges seen through snowfall: are they six
    patient oxen, heads down, battering open the wind
With their shoulders? Behind them, two men,
    shrunken in the white paths the animals break,
Stumble forward toward a horizon that recedes
    as they approach the Gate of Heaven,
That persistent mirage, that miracle. Decorated
    with tattered scarves, the animals refuse
To think. They put one hoof forward, then another,
    dragging their masters farther into the failing twilight.

CHRISTENING SONG

In this forest nothing lives, not even the forest.
    Its sky is sublimely colorless. The old man and woman
Toiling up a rocky slope to the crest of a minor mountain
    are insensible to whether clouds occlude the sun
Or whether there simply is no sun, only diffuse sourceless light.
    And they left that region behind them and ascended
To the great æons of the rulers and came before their veils
    and their gates, shining most exceedingly.
Beyond this border, another life is constantly unconcealed.

FRAGMENT OF A PERPETUALLY
UNFINISHED FIELD GUIDE

The snake understands that shadows are pieces of a night
　　broken apart by telephone poles and fence posts.
He carries one weightless fragment beneath him to protect his heart
　　inside its moveable pericardium, and another near his brain
Where it unfolds its tapestry of constellations—the adder, the dragon—
　　as a reminder of the insignificance of suns, and the origin
Of the firmament in the random shifting of invisible scales.

VICTIMS OF THE WEDDING 12
Window in a Cul-de-Sac

That landscape had been damaged; there were scars. The man and the woman walked out in the early morning and went to work with spading forks and hoes. By midmorning all evidence of the war had been smoothed over; by lunchtime, there were new gardens everywhere: herbs grew on the sites of foxholes, a burnt-out half-track provided the structure for a raised vegetable bed; there were flowers growing along the boundaries of no man's land.

It's interesting, the angel said, *how easily humans absorb history and remake it as if it had never happened. You'd think they'd wear out with it.*

It's different for them than for you and me, the daemon said, *they are able to forget because they are capable of ecstasy.*

BLOODFLOWER SERMON

The wind has windflowers, the sea anemones,
    death its endless procession of white bouquets.
We homeless ones circle a field in the guise of nightshade,
    absent our own blossoming. We nameless ones drop
No petals on the sandstone patio. A turbulent shaft of light
    strips us down to our essence and beats us raw.
What chance did we ever have, Great Ones, to be anything
    but planted in tilth in the end, and sentenced to calcium?

SEROTONIN

Long time we journeyed, not beaching on the foam
    at Ellis Island or on the gray firmament of Brooklyn Heights.
A curse had fallen on us, cast by no one. *No blame,*
    the Book of Changes said, and *mirabile dictu,*
There was none: just a great expanse of bile-black ocean
    adrift with rotting haddock and Styrofoam.
The crew collapsed on the gull-fouled deck, licking salt
    from each other's bellies, oblivious that all we had to do
Was climb the mainmast, tear a hole in the sky, arise, and fly on.

RX

That was a harsh, dark gift; no one wanted it, but it sustained them
   through the suppurations, vomiting, and delirium
Which many were convinced were *caused* by what they were given.
   For some, it was the true, pure cure; for others it was a poison
That might heal them despite itself and them, or might destroy them.
   But there was such a plague on the land—so virulent and disgusting—
That sooner or later everyone would be brought to the point of trying it.
   There was the smoking cityscape, shop windows smashed, subways deserted,
And I, numinous I, was the carrier, with my medical kit, and my one filthy syringe,
   and that chemical poetry that in the end they would kill me to possess.

VICTIMS OF THE WEDDING 13
In a Corner, the Spoor of a Large Animal

The woman waited. The man slept. Outside the big wind detonated across the ocean, and the small broken ship was scattered even farther up and down the shore, its masts shattering to kindling. The woman walked by the water, gathering the bits of boat, carrying them up to her woodpile. The ship that had carried him warmed the house for them, burning. The burning ship invisible behind the woodstove's window: the ship and all it contained, all it conveyed.

YOU HAD STUDIED ENGLISH AS A CHILD
IN ANOTHER COUNTRY

Before, our language churned goats' milk in the stinking hut.
    It parsed contracts in offices of strip malls, negotiated
Between wheat and the surfaces of grinding stones,
    graveyards and bulldozers, lepers and healing, girls
And field hockey lessons, execution and dismemberment.
    Before, our language demanded an after. Instead an *I*
Emerges now among the others, lonely as a clichéd Adam:
    First person. Singular. Present. Tense. Past perfect.

BUT A MORNING STAR

Those years they took to making love in the early morning
    before even the birds were awake, before the hound
Who snored in the garden could shake off his houndish dreaming
    and bay the constellations home. For now, this was the cusp,
And after, she would sleep, and he would dress and go down—
    in ordinary time not old or young, but in other systems
Neither had yet been born, or one of them was dying in a muddy trench
    while artillery pounded the mainland. When the war is over,
When the crisis of birth has made its peace, when ceremonies
    of passage are complete, and the hound is a heap of bones
Gnawed by hounds in the garden, there will still be the early morning.

WAR IN THE AGE OF PASTORAL

That whitewashed town, its buildings scattered
    down the valley at the foot of a black mountain—
Remember how delphinium flooded the gardens
    the day we arrived, how toxic the flowers were,
How lovers on the boulevard choked on the vapors
    as churches burned, how well we could see
Even the smallest details incised on the screen of our sensors,
    how incense rose from the targets as we sighted down.
After, we spent our lives deciding: is it right to wonder
    whether the juxtaposition of *delphinium* and *poison*
Is rhetorically shameless, like lyric propaganda,
    or whether it would have been worse
To leave the lovers drinking champagne in the park
    watched by sheep in the shade of silos
Where the keepers of missiles played dice in the underworld,
    the future depending on the mindless rolling of bones.

VICTIMS OF THE WEDDING 14
Chamber with Music and the Stink of the Bull

There were many children in the meadow on the hill. The man and woman had been fertile, and the children took the meadow like an invading army, in rags if they were wearing clothes at all, feral, lean, their eyes bright with hunger, their play, such as it was, like the play of young jackals, but each held an old spiral-bound notebook in his or her dirty hand, with the nub of a pencil attached to it by a length of greasy string. They moved across the meadow from every direction under a waning late autumn sun, as if they came there by pre-arrangement, as if there were a purpose in their convergence, a destination.

At the center of the meadow the angel was on all fours; behind the angel, the daemon mounted and entered, though just what angelic orifice received him or her it is difficult to say. As neither creature was permanently gendered, all the apparatus was nonce and, so to speak, home-made.

I still fail to see the pleasure in this, or any other purpose, the angel complained.

You still aren't doing it right, the daemon replied, laying another stripe on the angel's buttocks with a golden cat-o-nine-tails. *Haven't you watched the humans enough yet to understand?*

Evidently not, the angel muttered, changing, through a mystical force of will, the nether configuration to resemble yet more closely what humankind had revealed. *Perhaps we need more ichor, or some ectoplasm.*

Keep trying, the daemon grunted.

So distracted were the mystical pair that they failed to notice the sharp-toothed children surround them. They moved as quietly as ferrets through the grass and took up positions at all degrees around their objective. When they all were ready, they opened their notebooks and began to draw the most beautiful, accurate, and obscene illustrations of what they observed.

PANDROL JACKSON

Along a derelict railroad, abandoned machinery takes
    its last tour of duty toward rust. Another town is stalling.
Another house smolders with rot while a television rages.
    Crows patrol banked cinders beside a landfill with a sign:
No Dumping. We were Jews in Austria. No, we spoke German
    in Czechoslovakia—by order of the Alliance, we filed
Into a railroad car and died. No, we were black in Arkansas.
    Here is a filthy contraption, like a grim lawn mower
With flanged iron wheels, *Pandrol Jackson* in blue paint
    on its rotted housing: a rail grinder, used to polish steel
To brilliance, forgotten here as after the Rapture. And the carcass
    of a boxcar warps just down the track, groaning with a cargo of bones.

UNMANNED

Wood columns, verandah, a fanlight.
    Wicker. Ferns. A pile of bones
Next to the dog's bed radiates twilight.
    In the curdling sky, shadows drone
Their numinous presence and zero in.
    Oak planks sawed by prisoners
Warp infinitesimally toward the pure
    condition of dust. All possible pleasure
Has been accounted for. Down the street,
    In every window, disembodied lights appear,
And an X of blood targets every door.

THE INQUISITION

Along the endless hallway (can infinity be concrete?
    these walls are concrete block) leaning on a walker,
Demanding the worn-out knee (now refitted with steel
    from a cruel dimension not of bone and blood)
To drag the body with it, all this motion a tribute
    to the pure will to Be: like that Cathar spared
His right eye by the Inquisitor so that he might lead
    the other 99 less lucky over the lovely landscape
Of the summer-struck Midi, under the all-seeing, indifferent
    gaze of God, beyond, to the idea of home.

VICTIMS OF THE WEDDING 15
Glimpse of an Unattainable Exit

When he woke up, the man thought he was reborn, and then he thought he had dreamed the great storm. What would he have been doing on a ship at all, much less being the captain of one? And the room he woke in was both strange to him and familiar. He seemed to remember being carried. Who would have carried him, from where, and why? He felt weak, but only from hunger; he was hungry. He desired. But when the woman appeared in front of him—had she stepped out of a shadow?—he knelt in front of her. She put her hand on his head. He thought she would ask him to rise, but she did not: she held him there with a power he did not understand, but to which he gladly acceded. He was in her domain.

Doesn't he know all he has to do is stand up? the angel said. *She's not preventing him.*

He's choosing, the daemon said. *Angels always have difficulty comprehending the nature and significance of human choosing.*

Angels never make choices, the angel said. *Or, well, one did, and that is why the rest of us don't.*

THE GREAT WATER

The Oracle throws her yarrow stalks. Where they fall
    is defined as Fate. Why not? When the drunk
Truck driver hits a bridge abutment and levitates
    through his own windshield, that portal
Of vision, his load of logs flies too. If he wakes
    barely injured, a chaos of stripped pine boles
Around him, does he survive because he's blessed?
    Divine Providence, he says. Now he lives
Another life. He speaks in tongues. *Thunder*
    under the lake: the Oracle casts her runes.
The superior one at nightfall re-enters the Book of Changes.

VANISHING POINT

In the great valley between Hwando and Yazoo City,
    laborers tend opium poppies and cotton,
Dying of yellow fever. But on the heights, there is a calm
    incense of roasting pork, a delicate mist of flesh
Lovers stroll through to the platform at cliff's edge
    Where they gaze down like diligent scholars
At a landscape falsified precisely for their pleasure.
    From there, a faint pentatonic music skirls
Up from the valley floor, where we overseers hone
    blue notes from invisible instruments stroked
With the abrasive bow of coal smoke and acid rain.

PUSH

Push, the great voice commands, and a body falls
    into the midwife's hands. Outside, horns
Fanfare a fender bender, sirens slicing the morning,
    nobody tied to the mast. *Push,* and the innocent
Clouds vomit thunder. *Push,* and a blister of plasma
    erupts the Big Bang. The baby cries. *Push,*
And milk exfoliates into the nipple. *Push,* and the bright
    dagger slides into Caesar's left kidney. *Push*
Says the sign on the hotel door where the lovers stumble
    into a grand old lobby. Outside the city staggers
And the river tumbles. *Push,* says the woman, wrapping
    her legs around him, and he does, and the sperm push in.

VICTIMS OF THE WEDDING 16
Hallway with Collapsing Roof

Having made his choice, the man turned and saw a landscape transformed. Gouts of bloody cloud rose into the sky, pillars of smoke and flame; bombs fell from unseen incunabula in the vortex of the firmament. He looked again and saw the body of the woman, pierced by a splintered two-by-four from the frame of the demolished house, framed in a bed of hibiscus; the angel and the daemon too had been torn to fragments by the maelstrom, and their essences flung across the moonlit lawn. He looked skyward and saw his own disintegration descending like a flaming airship from the black sky.

IMPERIAL

There are few still standing now who remember
    when they sold Prince Albert in a can.
He was beautifully dressed, a fine trope of a man,
    with a beard, and a nose, and slender
As the riding crop the Queen used to punish him
    when he forgot his place—inside the oblong tin
Farmers bought in country stores: *imperially thin*
    like Richard Cory in the famous poem.
They were near contemporaries. But you can't imagine
    the Prince Consort doing himself in.
In my mind he rides close to the hearts of men
    in work-shirt pockets; he ministers to the ways
Of colonials blind to the pressure of Victoria's corset stays.

WHEN FAULKNER KILLED RILKE

The black cedar is edited from a nightmare,
    and the deconstructed oak
An outtake from a terrible dialogue
    between the earth and a lightning bolt.
Whoever you are, come out of your room.
    The mundane radiance of winter afternoon
Is replaying something you called *my life,*
    O numinous, O golden, etc. In the trailer
Parked forty years ago behind the brick plant,
    one of the ancients of the earth knocks back
Another bourbon. Rilke never wrote the word
    Mississippi. As far as Mississippi knows,
Rilke never wrote. Muddy water, impossible shore,
    which came first, the chicken or the road?

THE END OF RELIGION

Cursed are the galvanized, for rust
    is the ecstasy of entropy.
Cursed are the bleak, for theirs
    Is the wreckage of vision.
Two prophets walk into a bar: *What's*
    it gonna be? Two Buddhists
Walk into the void: *One with everything.*

VICTIMS OF THE WEDDING 17
Icarus Falls through the Roof of the Penultimate Chamber

If there is no earth, can the airliner be descending? Is the wedding party waiting? Will there be champagne in the void? Will there be a wedding band? In his spiral-bound notebook, the man is writing everything he knows with the stump of a pencil. *It is said a person is the sum of a life's choices. My choices have been random, and fated, and fatal, and so this is what I am.*

DISSIPATION LYRIC

A pillar of dust blown over the desert, a tower
   of smoke attended by crows and helicopters.
Starvation is a luxury; so is the fever of consumption.
   Acute, this drifting away, this nebulous abnegation.
Upturn the urn on the mesa's edge, unleash the caustic ash.
   The one who is leaving is already gone
In a brume of greasy smoke and star gas.

URN BURIAL

The mind of a cockroach in the body of a man,
    the body of a cockroach in a man's brain—
The alchemists understood how unlike things combine:
    Iron Curtain, Iron Age, Iron Horse, Iron Maiden.
So the iron fist descends dispassionately on the frangible skull
    of the one who will shortly lie in a mass grave.
But the bloody-handed one considers himself a slave
    of history, compelled by an insect will
To outlive apocalypse, whether fire, plague, or radiation,
    sending others on before him freed of the body
And its corrupt admixtures—oblivious to his own transformation
    to a lixivial husk in an urn, interred in honey.

SKANDALON

Plumed gods have their own agendas, and fly where they will at whatever
    speed they choose, being gods, being plumed, and strike the earthly air
as they choose, being choosers and not the chosen; but choosing can be
    their weakness, the chink in the godly adamantine, not quite so open
as the term "Achilles heel" connotes—demigods being oddball hybrids—but
    real enough. And so when this god, pimped out in his serpent form—

for the benefit, one supposes, of the masses—chose to turn and *see:*
    not to treat the human world as a slum of mortality, beneath his notice
but actually to *look*, it was his undoing; and what did the priest
    on his pyramid offer that so distracted an Eternal? The usual: a sacrifice,
but one so exquisite that even the cruel god was dazzled: on the altar
    above its pit of acidic flame a single butterfly, glamoured, etherized,

then meticulously dismembered, as the rapt god watched, with a knife
    of priestly obsidian itself shaped like a butterfly, the priest wielding
not only the knife but a lifetime of disciplined skill, and love for the god,
    and love for the butterfly, and a body odor so acrid
it made the priestly donkeys and all the gathered virgins retch—
    but gods are beyond that, their contempt for humankind is so refined

that anything of the body escapes them, which is what the priest knew
    as he carved his monarch's wings in a series of hierophantic gestures
that appeared to be an efficacious magic of indeterminate kind—so the god
    thought, for gods always think that way—but in fact were nothing
but a signal to his hidden assistants: and so when the trap was sprung
    the god was disempowered by a godly wonder of his own devising

And was turned, on a plinth of quartz, in one shrewd human stroke,
    into this stone being you see before you now, my children, one eye still
gazing at the deconstructed butterfly which now is millennia turned
    to dust, and the other eye, a perfect study in godly outrage, still fixed
on your hungry hearts, my children, hating each of you with a godly passion,
    and waiting, waiting forever if necessary, for that hatred's unveiling.

VICTIMS OF THE WEDDING 18
The Work of the Maker

Before time began, but after the last war, all the spirits were gathered in a great echoing vacuous space. They arranged themselves in a hierarchal circle, understanding without being told by anyone that they were about to be offered an opportunity, one which must be faced decisively and accomplished precisely, otherwise something as yet nameless and unknown would overtake that which had yet to be created. Before them appeared a large bin, painted drab green and spotted with rust, the mystic word DUMPSTER stenciled on its side. Inside, they all knew (again without being told), were objects, though in that time before objects existed that word had a dubious status.

One by one, in the order of their place in the great schematic, the spirits came forward, looked into the bin—which was practically speaking gazing into a future universe—and chose the thing that then became the destiny of his or her kind. First came the greatest of the demiurges, who chose a golden crown known as Kether, the topmost of the Sephirot of the Tree of Life; then came the archangels, who chose sundry wings and haloes; after them the multitudes of angels and seraphim and cherubim, who carted away robes and sandals and censors as if they were bargains at a yard sale. They were followed by the daemonic orders—djinn, foliots, devils of all kinds, Beelzebubs all, collectors of pitchforks and sulfuric vapors and the like. The gathering was multitudinous beyond counting, and the bin, though not as large as one might expect, seemed inexhaustible—setting a pattern for the future of miracles.

Still, as the ceremony proceeded and the gathered, after most of an eternity, dwindled, the last of the spirits approached the great receptacle. This of course was the spirit of humanity, last in everything, and least likewise. A meager wisp of a creature, the spirit of humanity had to borrow an ottoman from a sleepy Luciferian to stand on in order to reach the very rim of the bin.

When the spirit looked inside, it discovered to its surprise that the bin was neither empty (usually the kind of thing that happened to the spirit of humanity), nor containing merely a single rejected item (which is what long conditioning had led the spirit of humanity to think the most likely eventuality). To its surprise, it found there three things: a decaying brain, a bloody heart, and an old spiral-bound notebook, with the nub of a pencil attached to it by a length of greasy string. Horrified by the brain and disgusted by the heart—while only disappointed in the notebook—the spirit chose the latter.

A bolt of lightning split the sky, which before had been nonexistent, and—in punishment for having made the wrong choice yet again—the spirit of humanity was forced to take the heart and the brain as well.

A RECONCILIATION

And they were happy in the end, if by *happiness*
    you mean *everything was forgotten.*
Time had been deeply layered in their bodies
    like the ruins of Troy in a hill. Now the innocent
Cattle waged war on milkweed in a pasture,
    while a formation of geese wedged harmlessly
Into the evening air. What had they fought about
    endless years ago? Time clarifies nothing,
But buttresses of worked stone dissolve in its weightlessness.
    Nothing now to defend except their bodies,
Which survived, growing lighter and more translucent
    and more useless. In the night sky, stars convened
In images of gods and humans, watching for a sign
    of any remnant of passion, a recognition of blood
Transcendence: old Helen fucking ruined Menelaus.

DISCARD

CPSIA information can be obtained at www.ICGtesting.com
Printed in the USA
BVOW05s2034040914

365404BV00003B/213/P